Tick Tack Toe Game
by Art McGee

Table of Contents

1. Introduction

Thank you again for purchasing my Tick tack toe book, I hope you enjoy playing these game with your kids and friends.Because this is very exciting for you to play games together.This book will change your life, I put this book together for you to enjoy and have fun. Thank you for choosing my book.

2. Tick Tack Toe Game

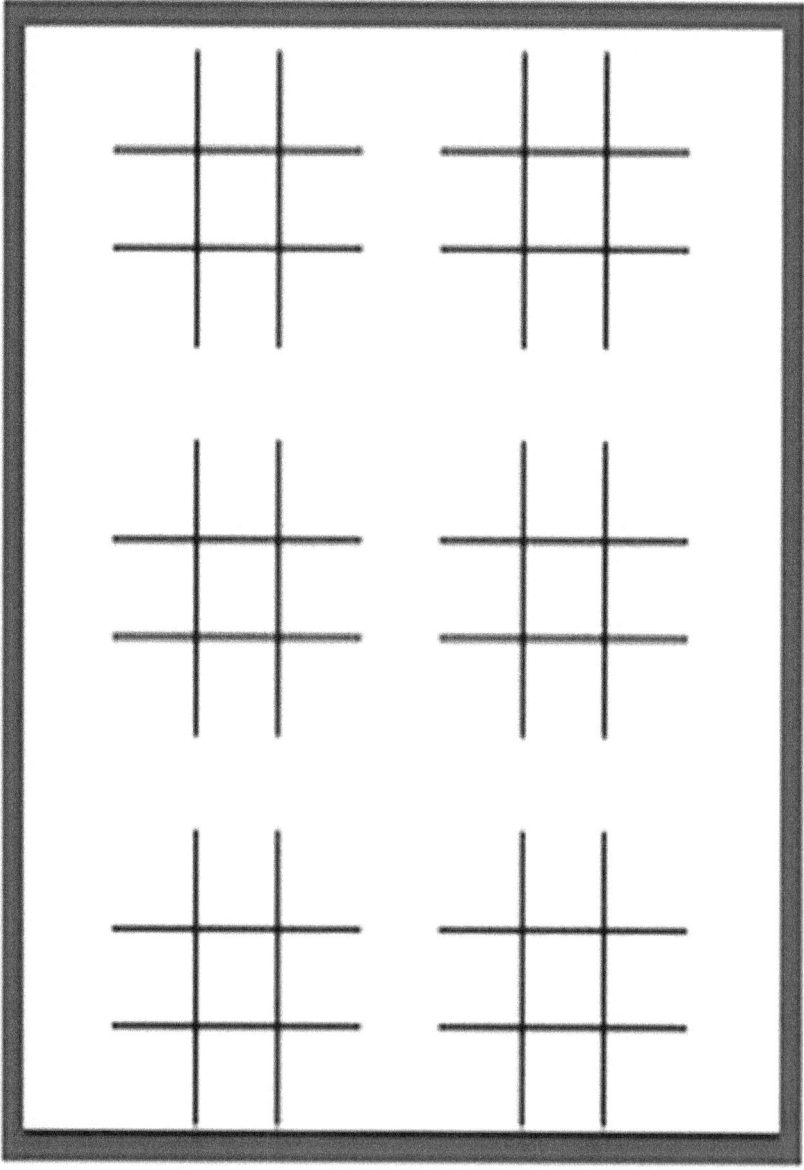

3. Tick Tack Toe Game

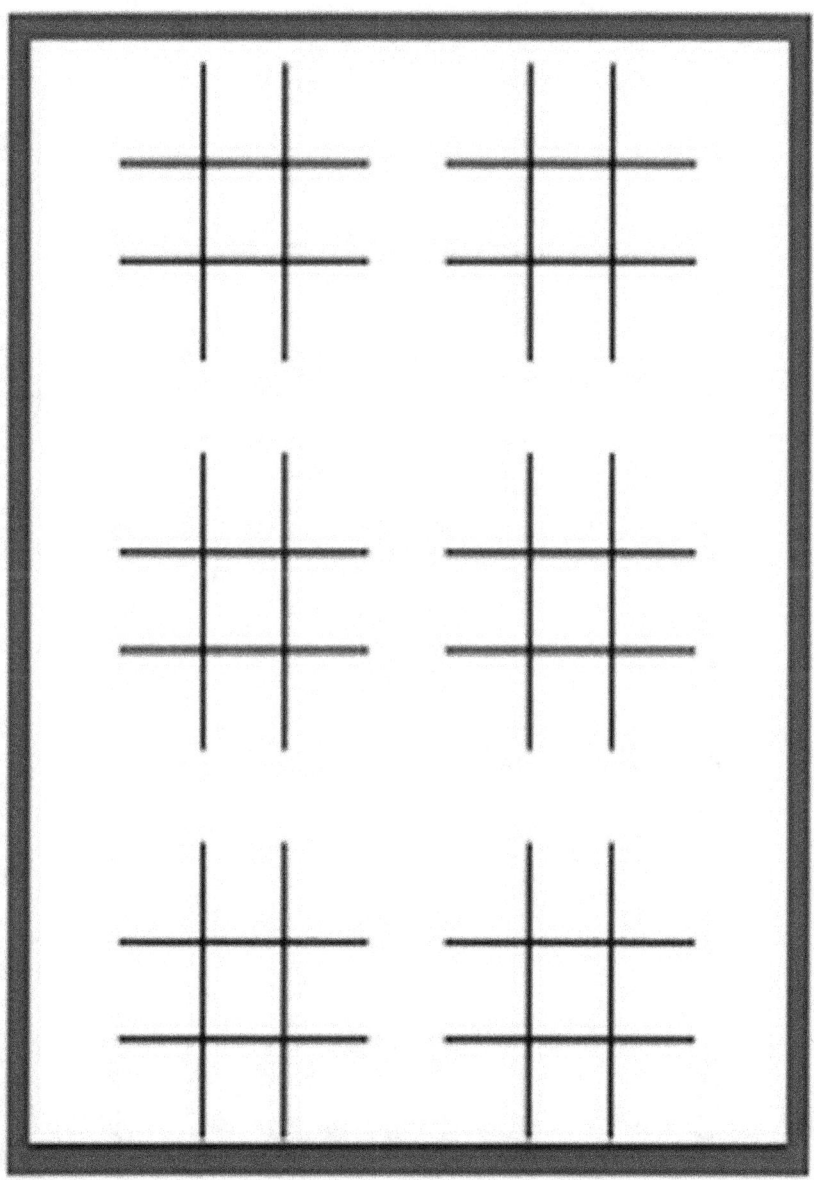

4. Tick Tack Toe Game

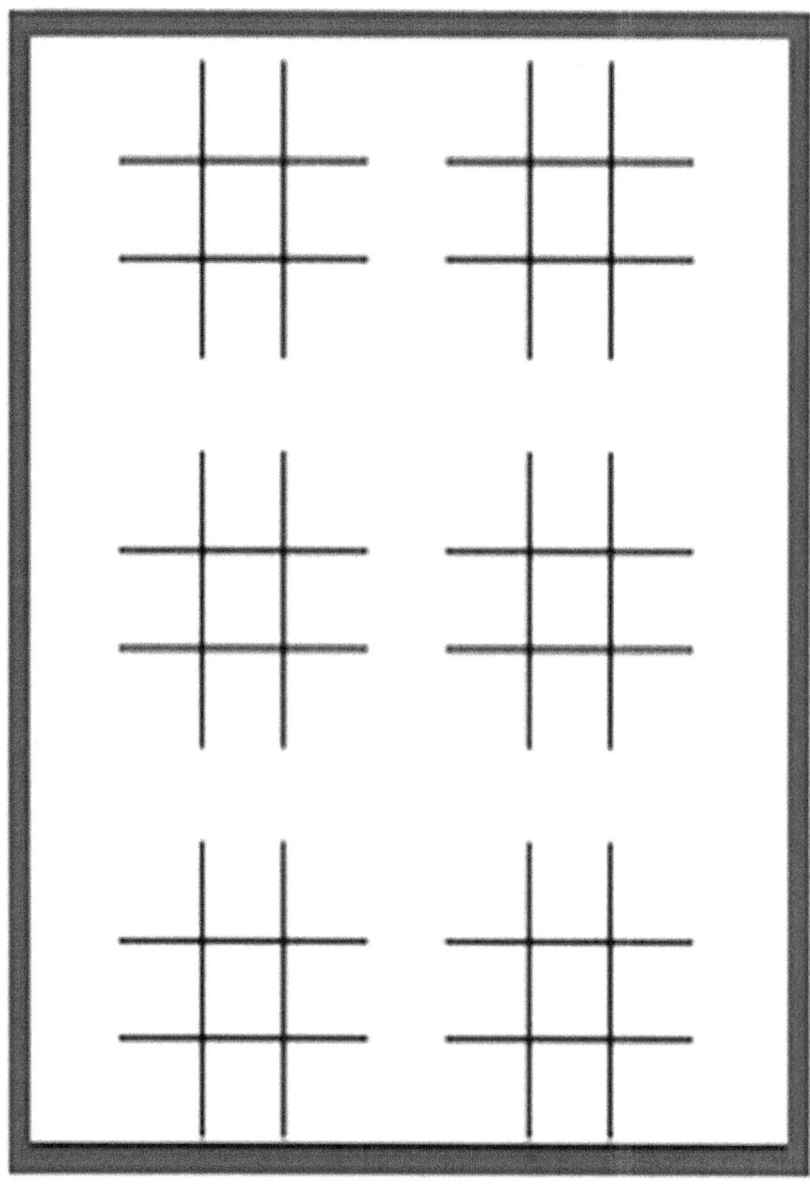

5. Tick Tack Toe Game

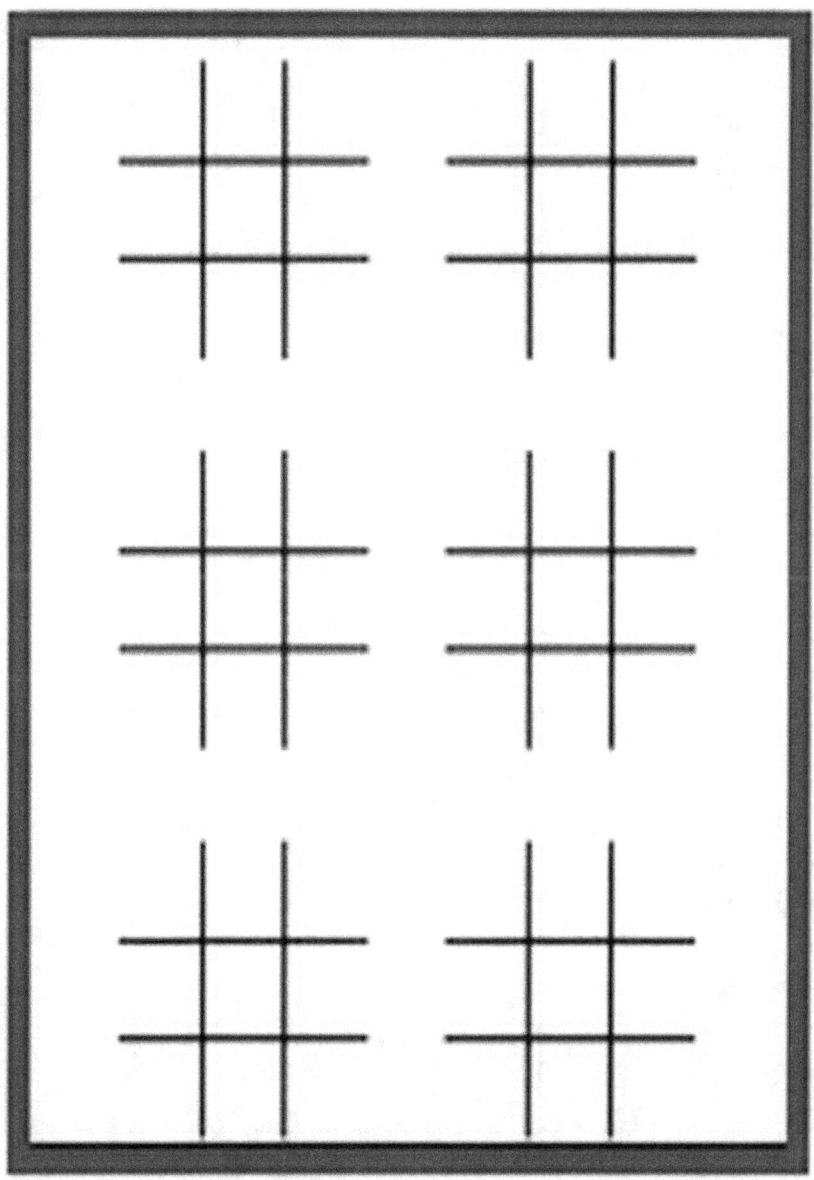

6. Tick Tack Toe Game

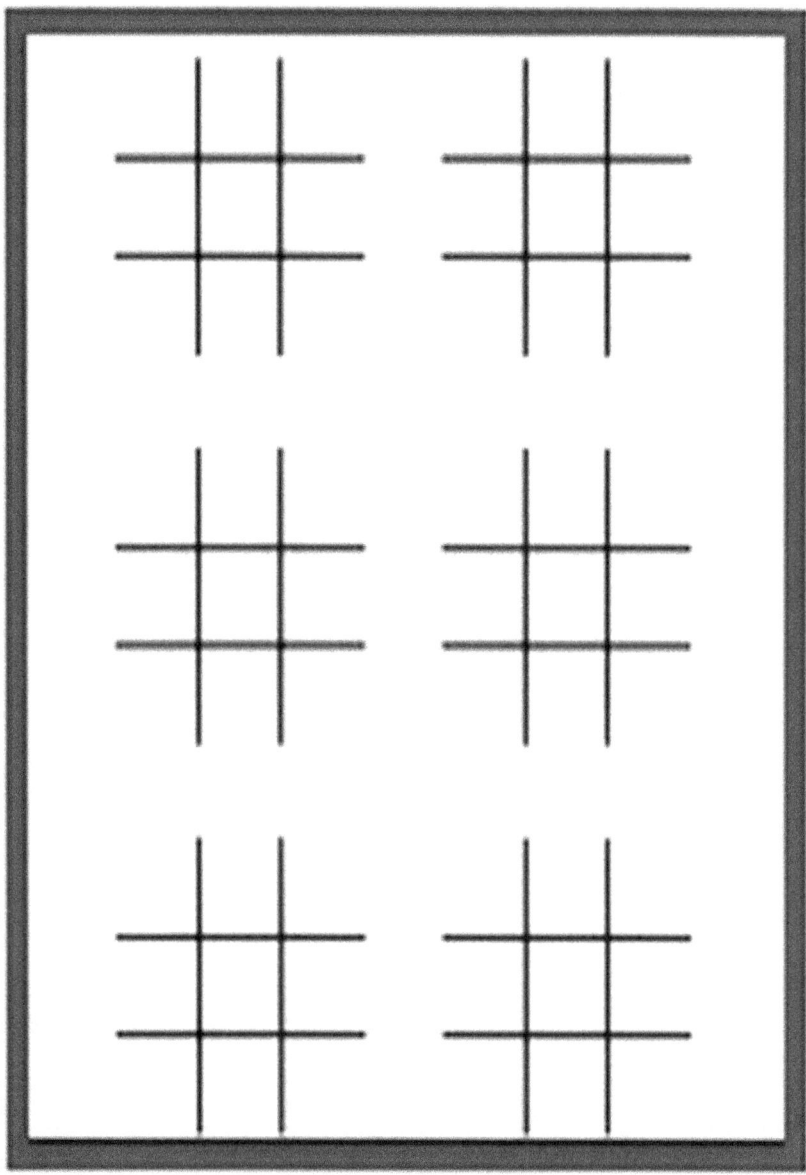

7. Tick Tack Toe Game

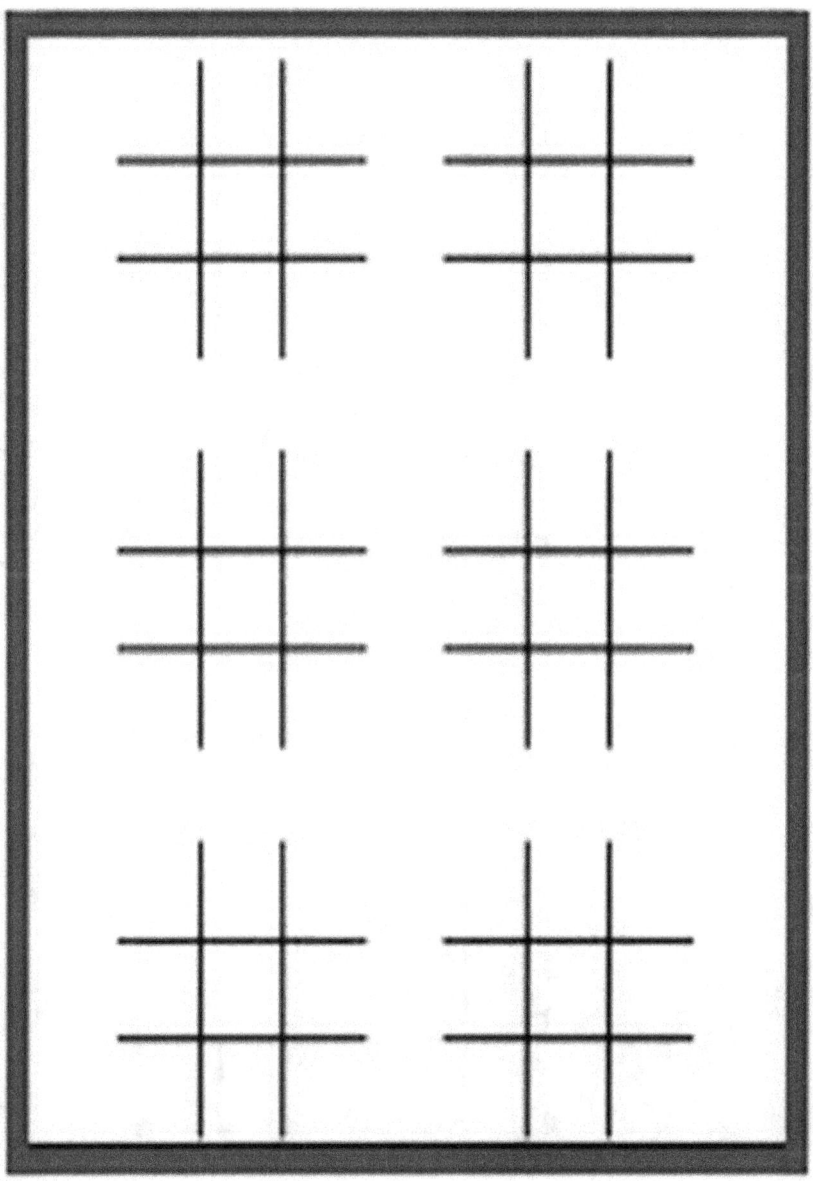

8. Tick Tack Toe Game

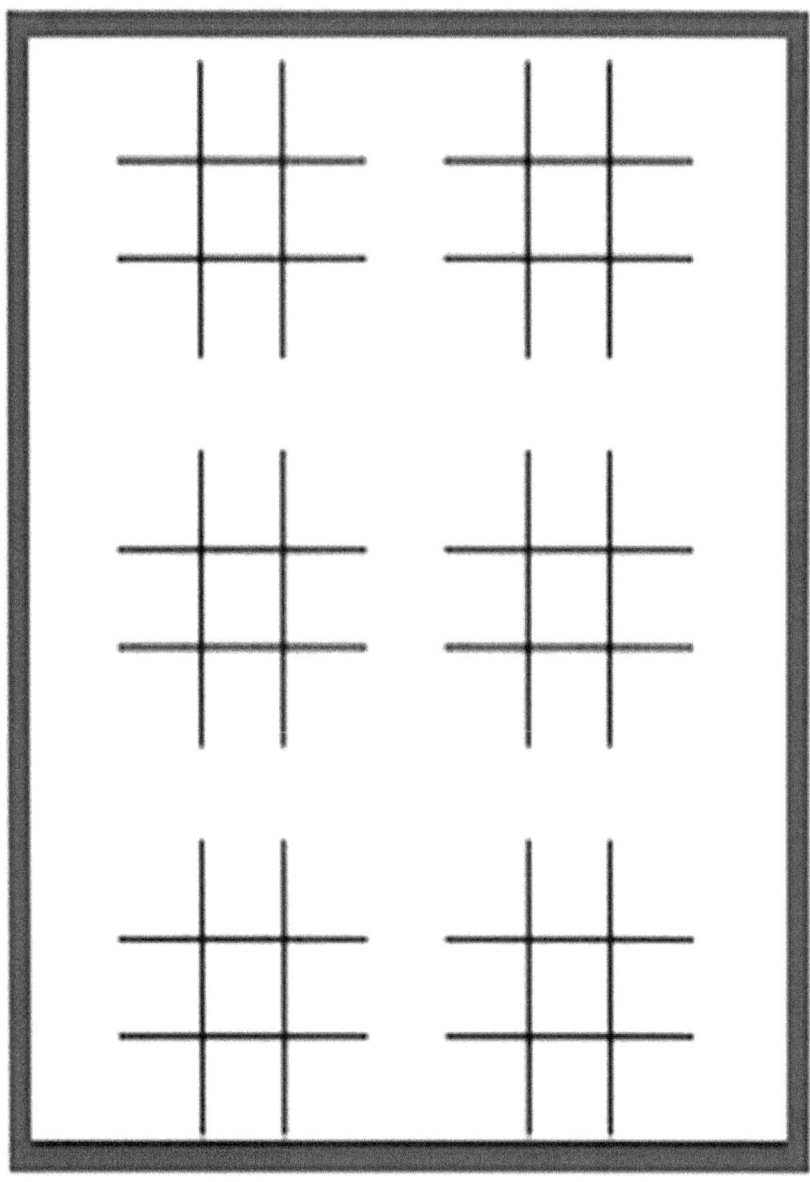

9. Tick Tack Toe Game

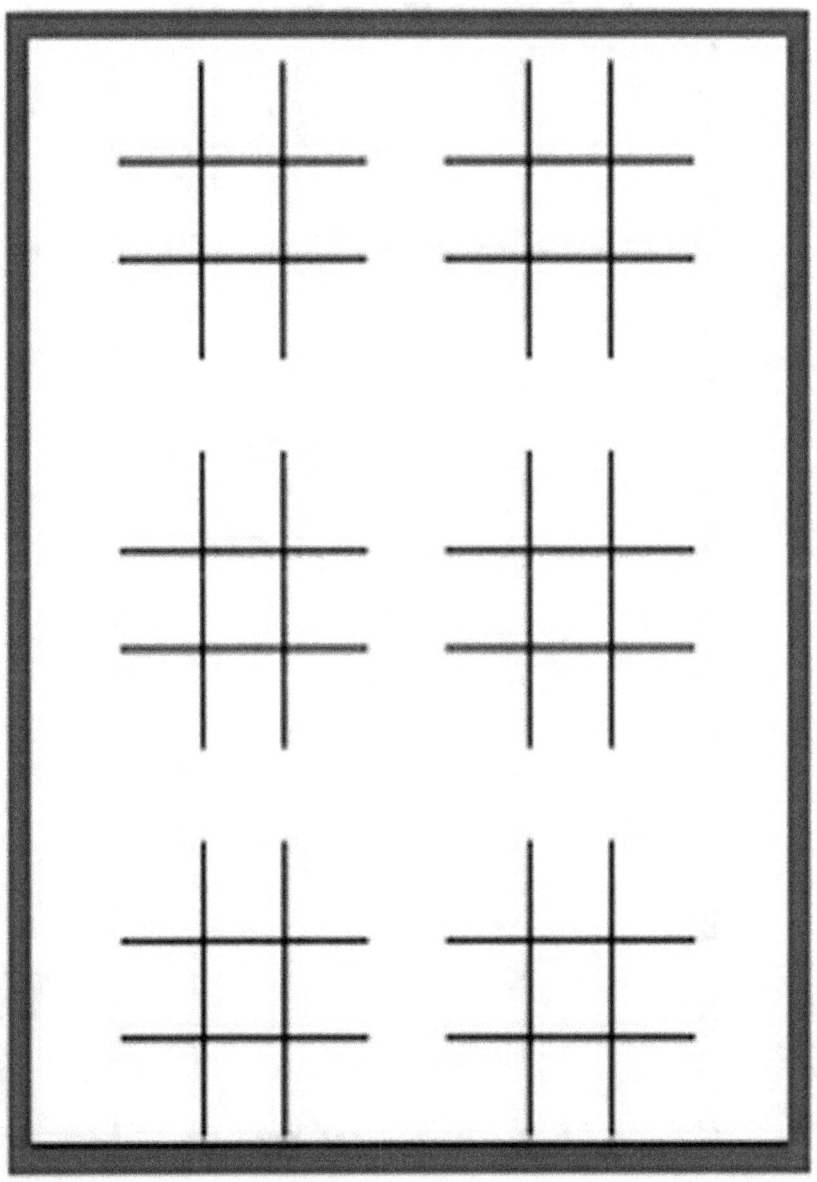

10. Tick Tack Toe Game

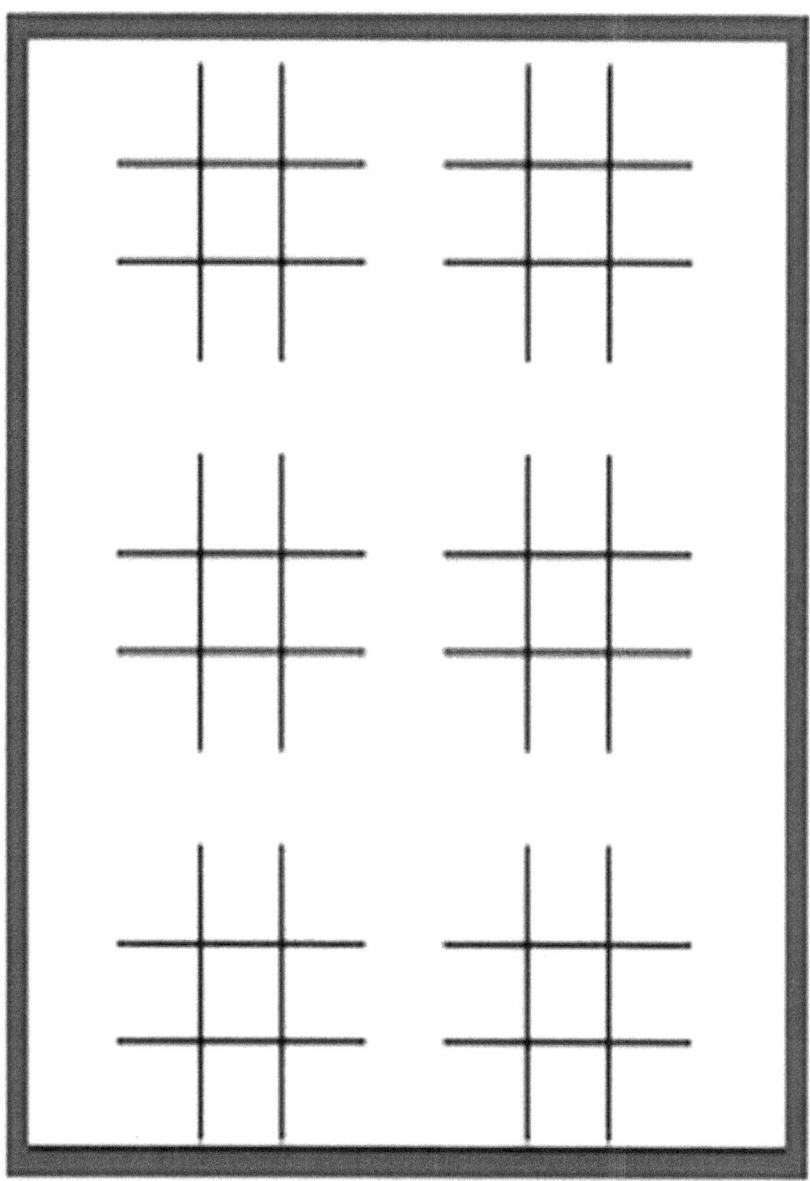

11. Tick Tack Toe Game

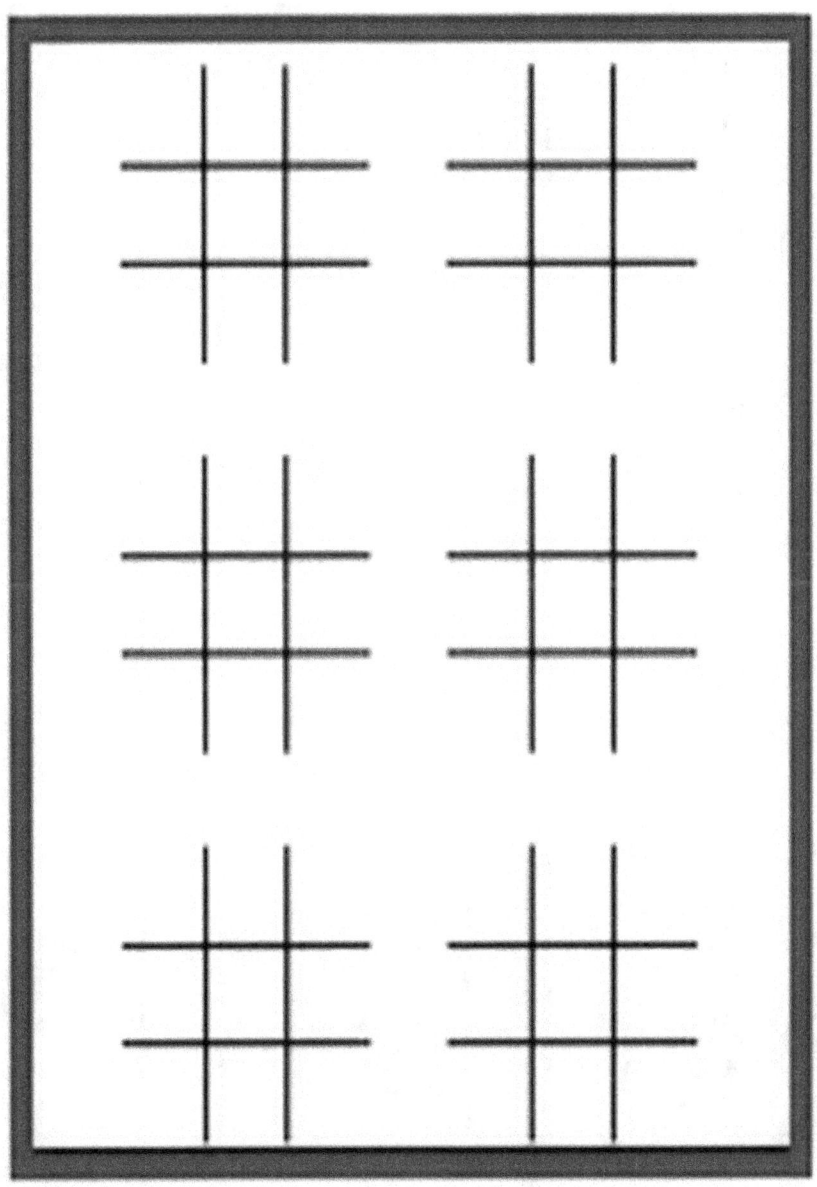

12. Tick Tack Toe Game

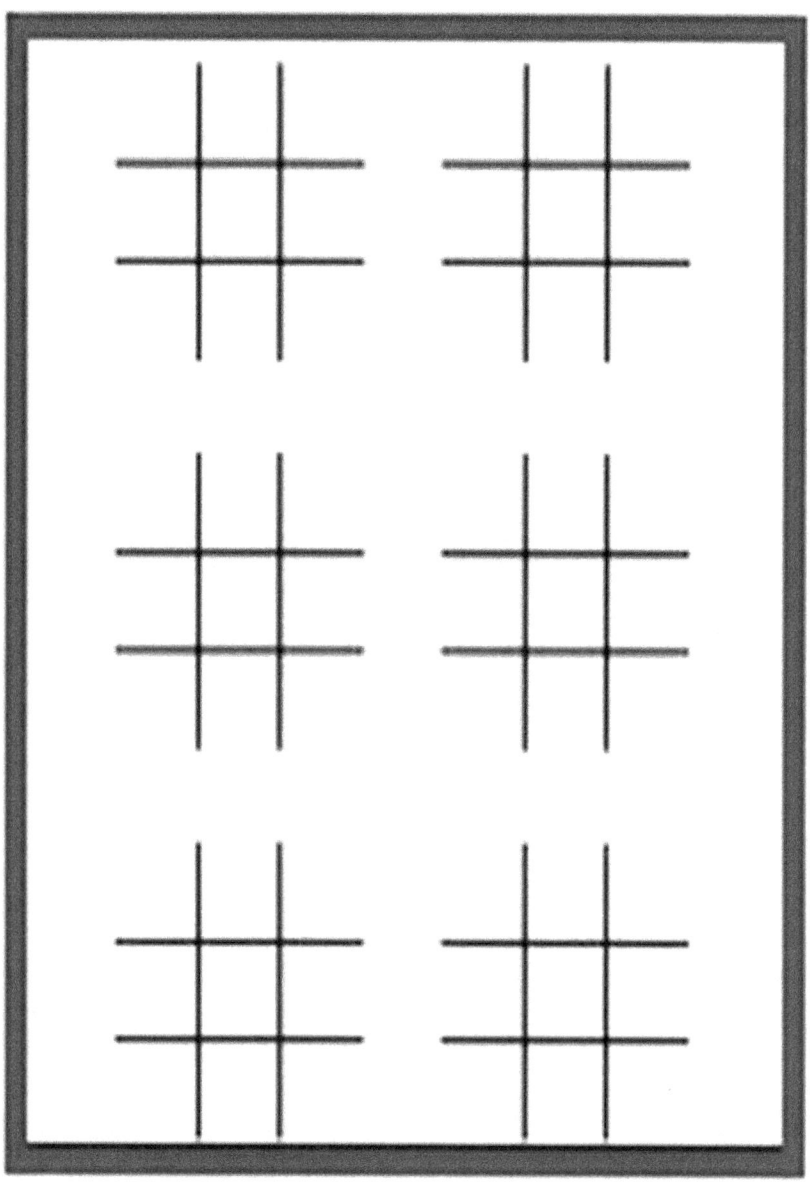

13. Tick Tack Toe Game

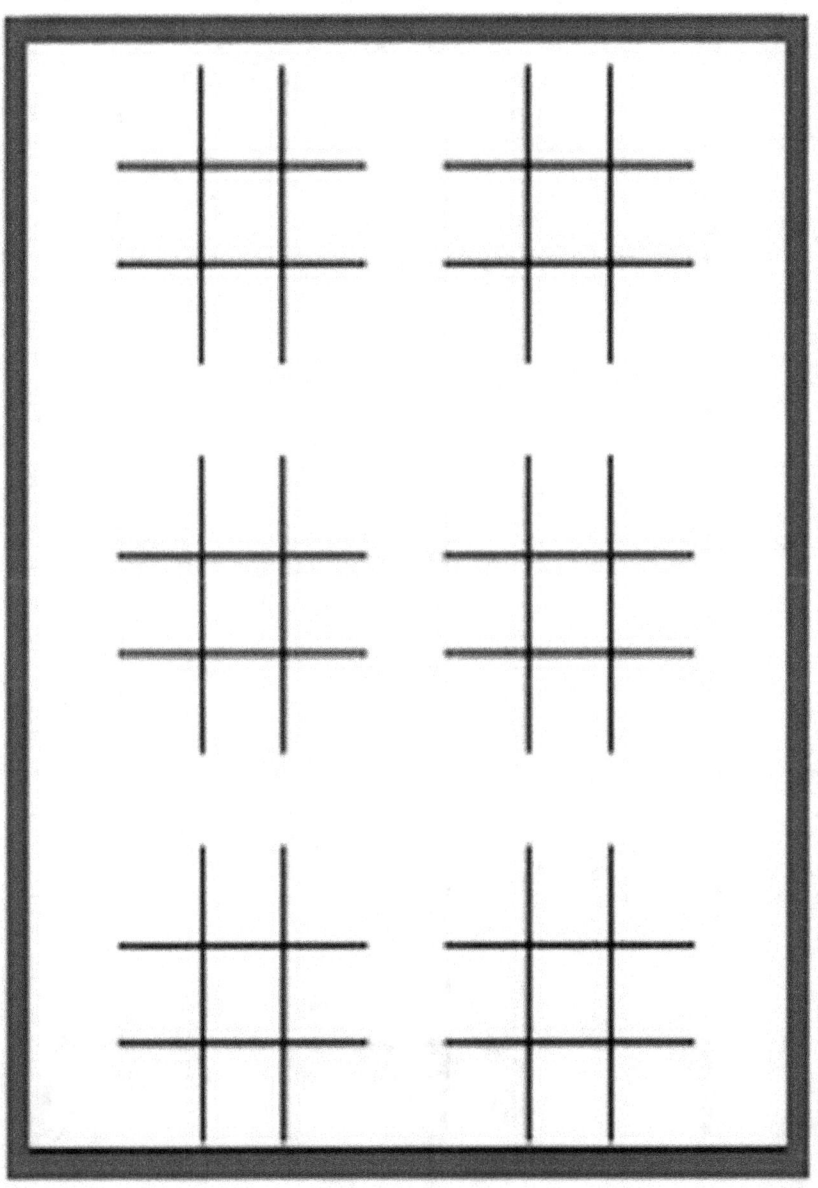

14. Tick Tack Toe Game

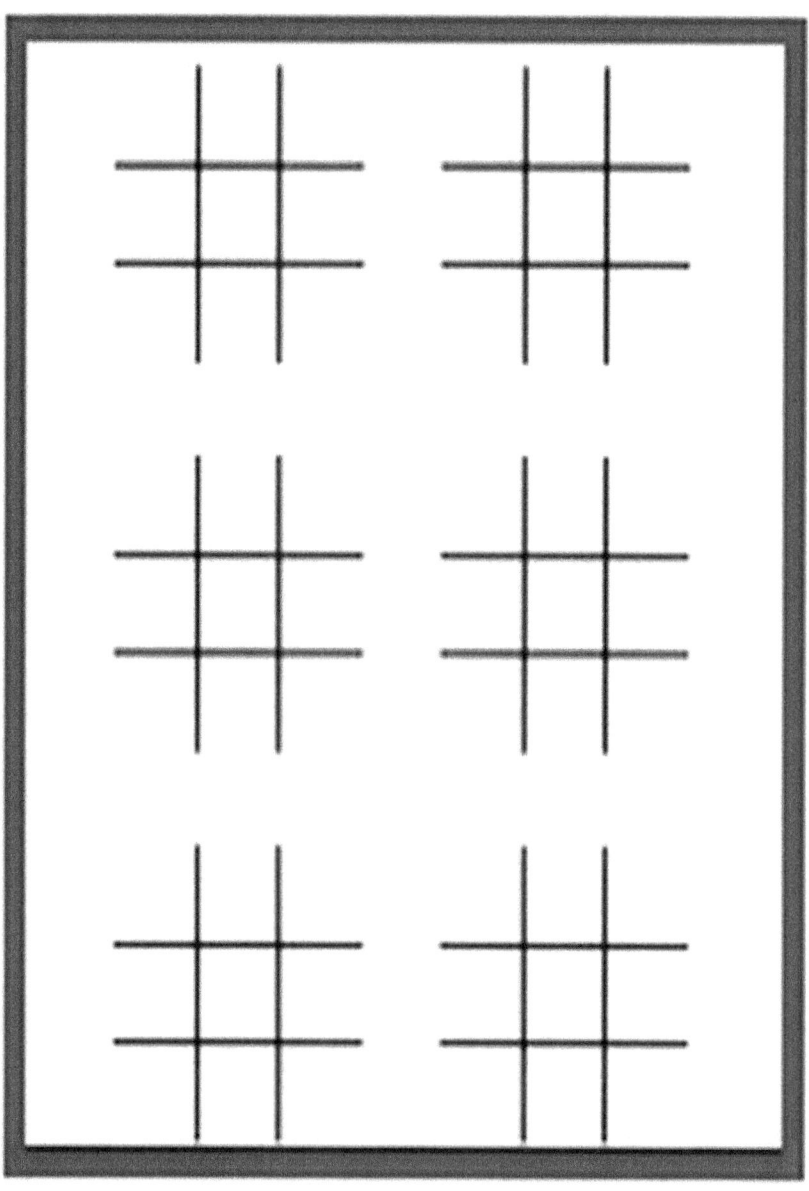

15. Tick Tack Toe Game

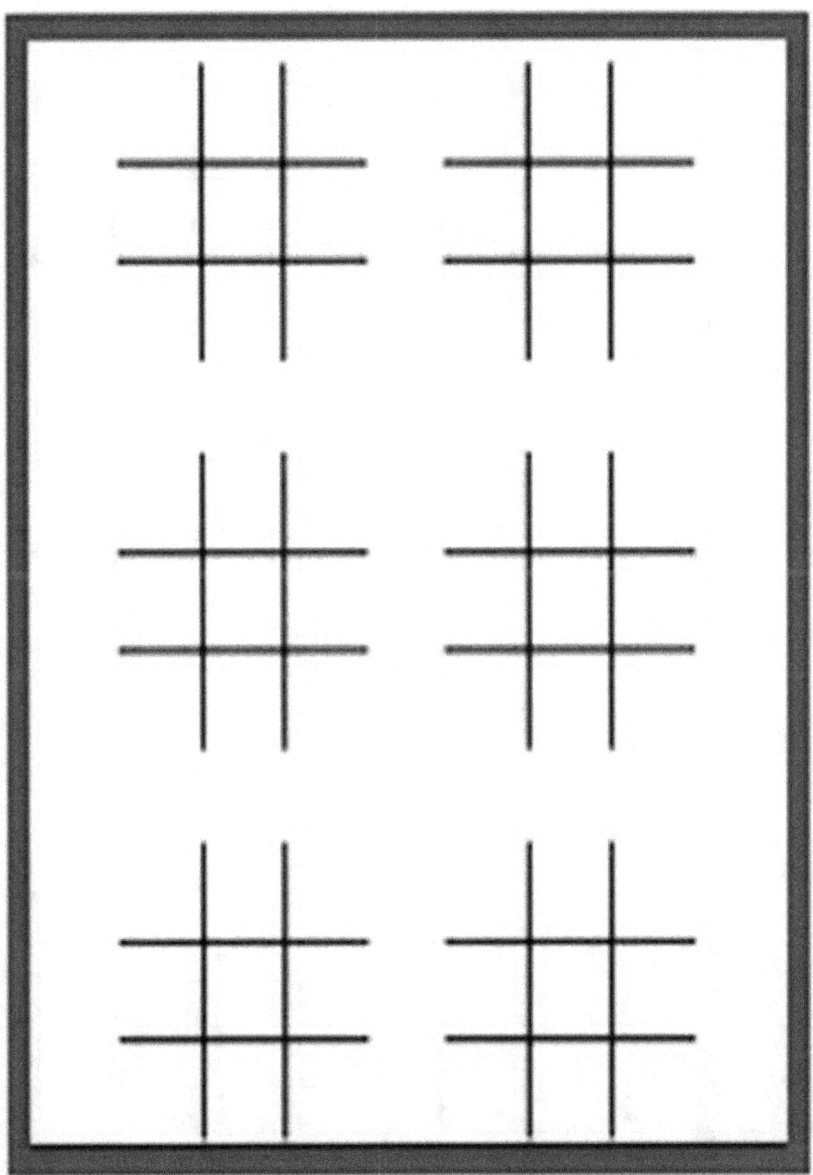

16. Tick Tack Toe Game

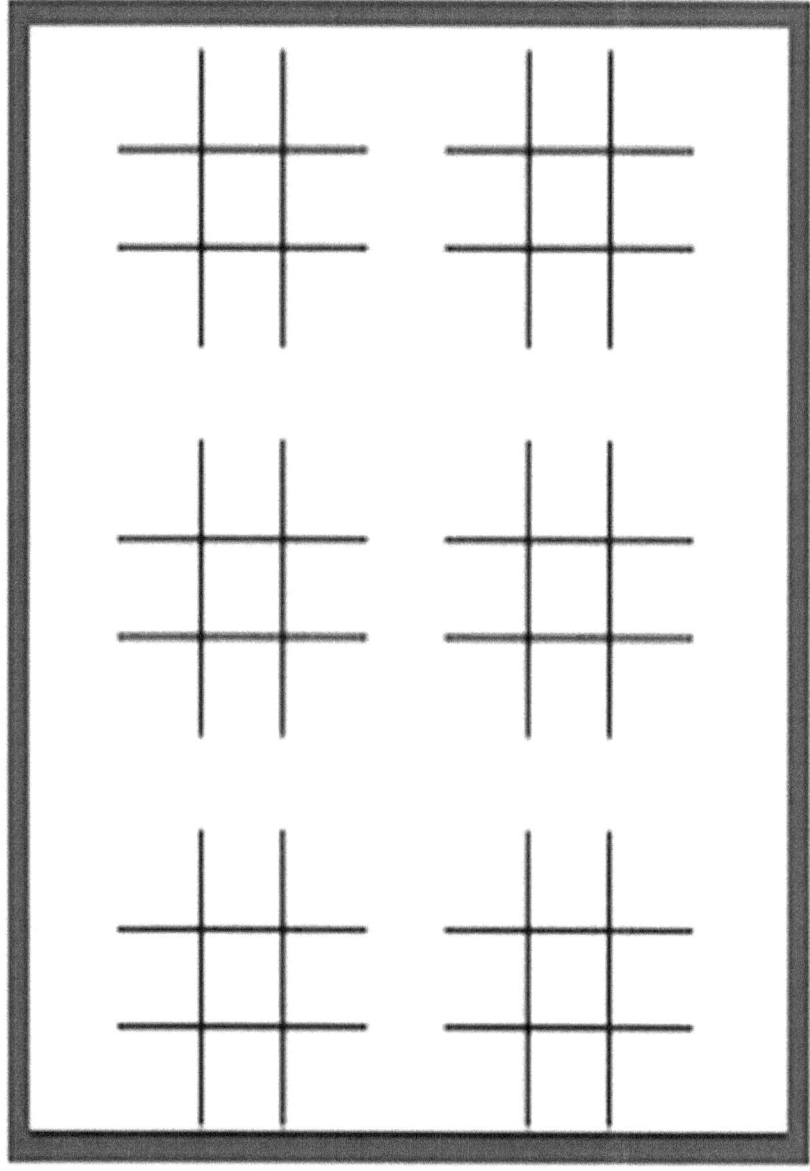

17. Tick Tack Toe Game

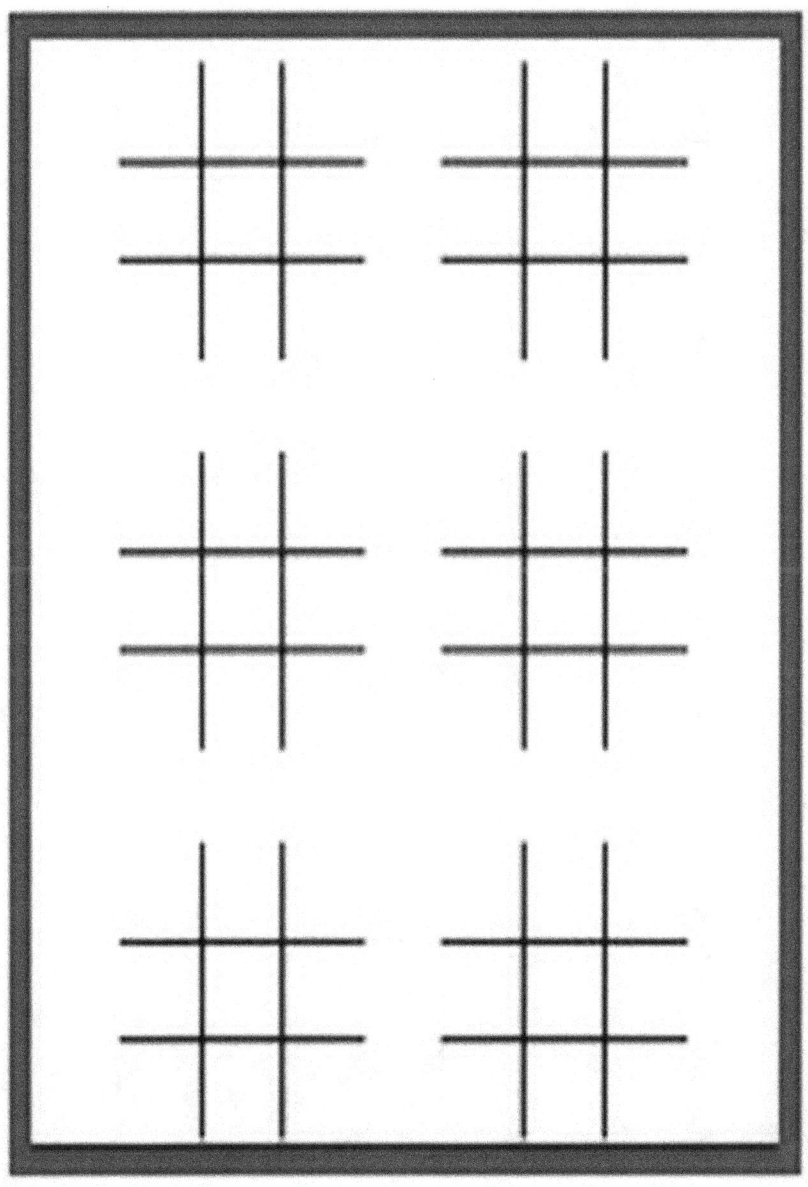

18. Tick Tack Toe Game

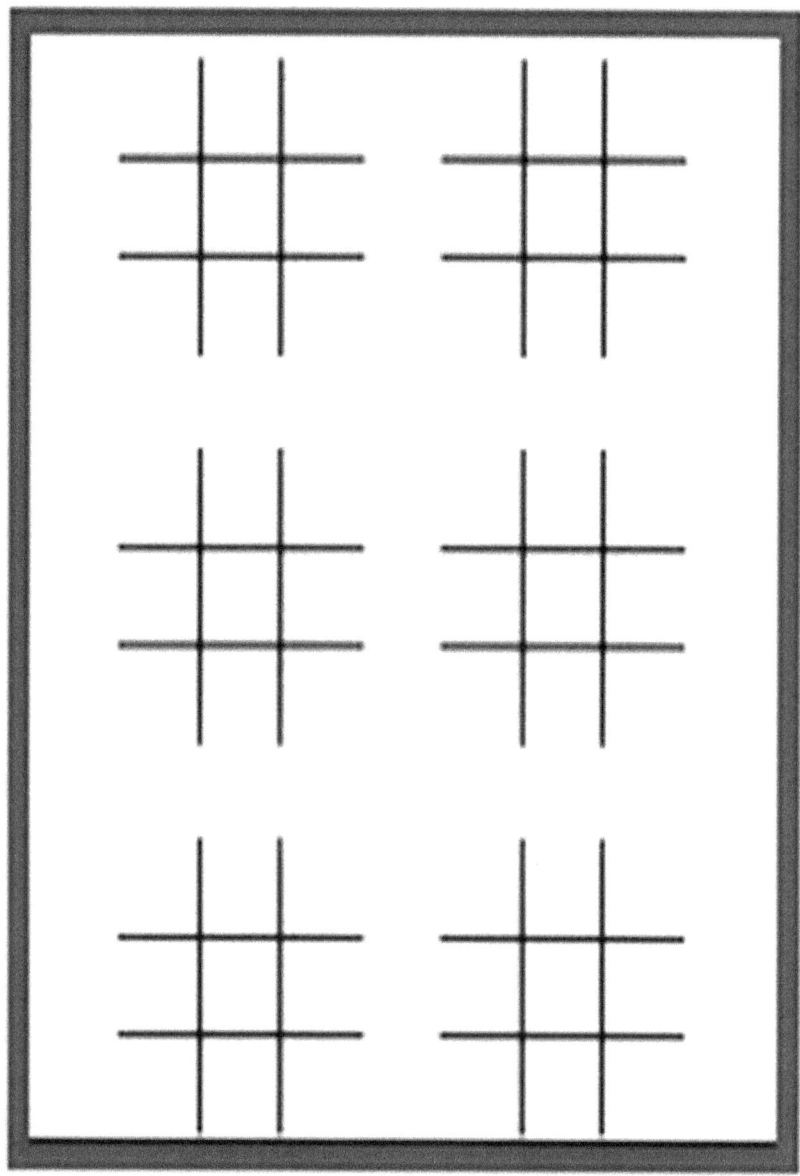

19. Tick Tack Toe Game

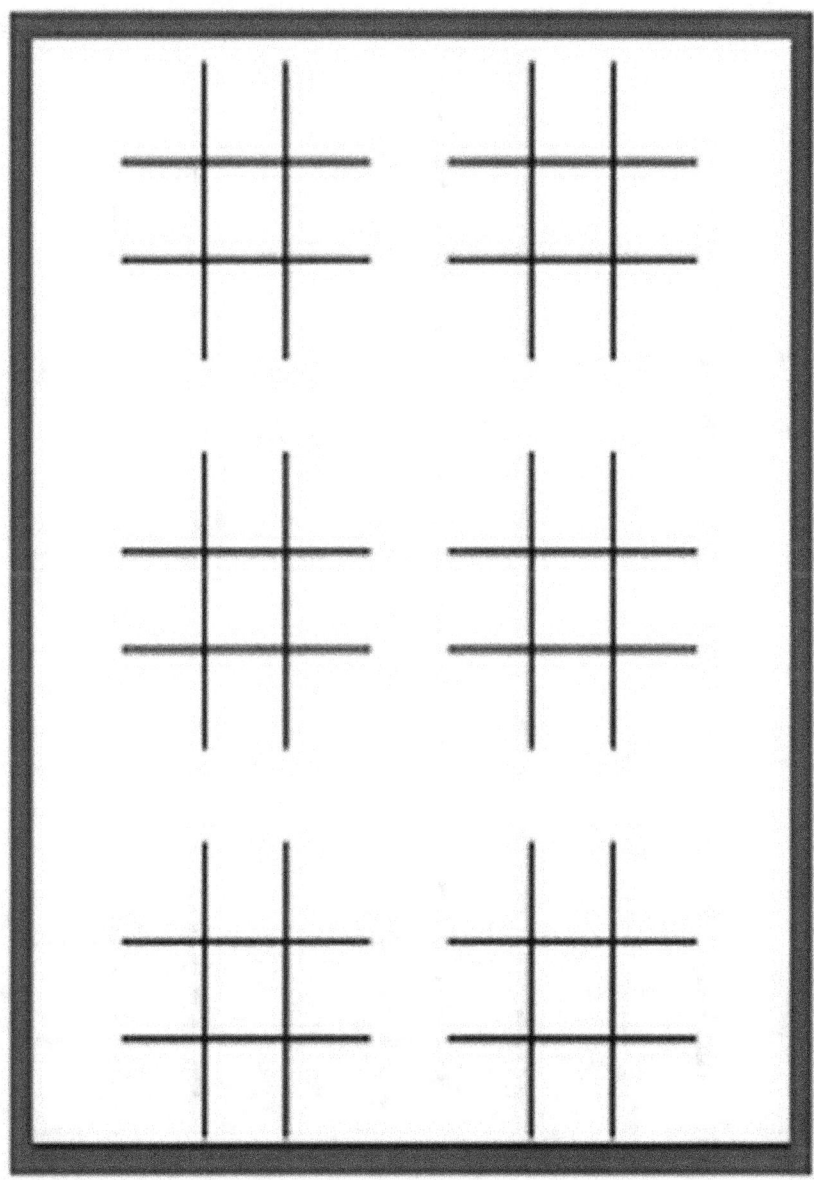

20. Tick Tack Toe Game

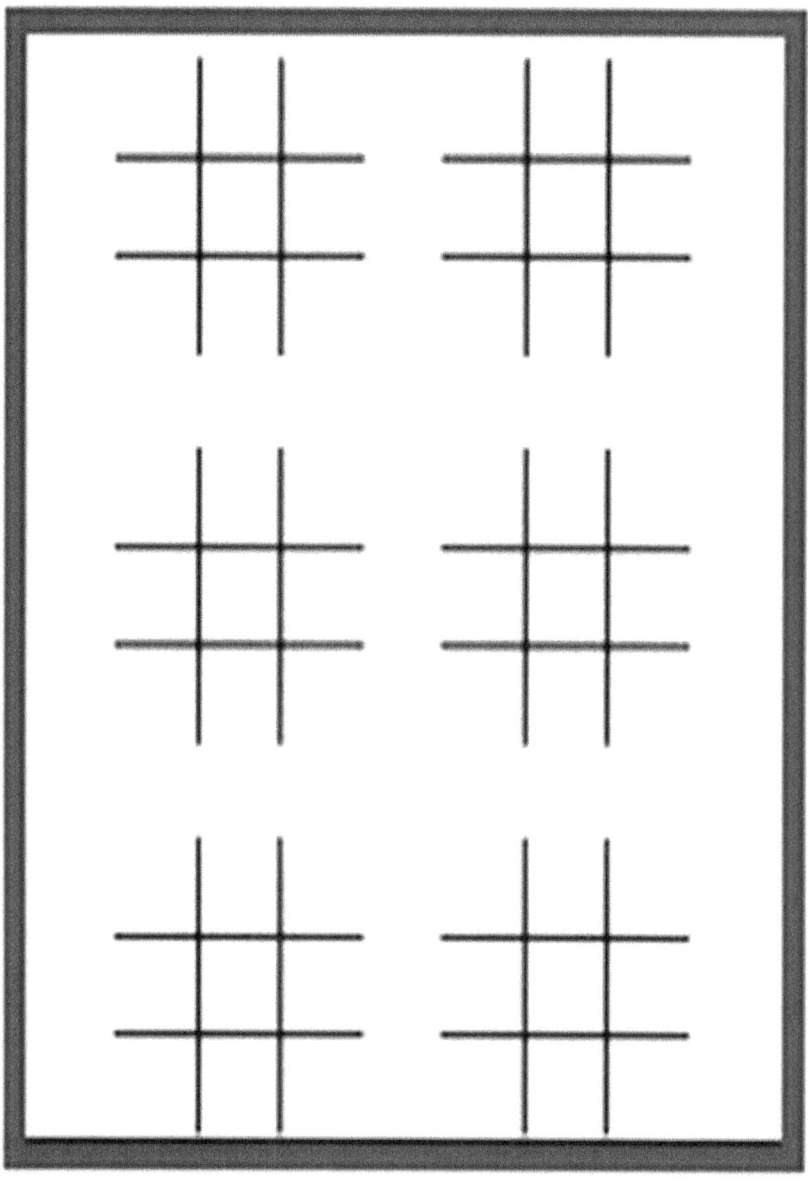

21. Tick Tack Toe Game

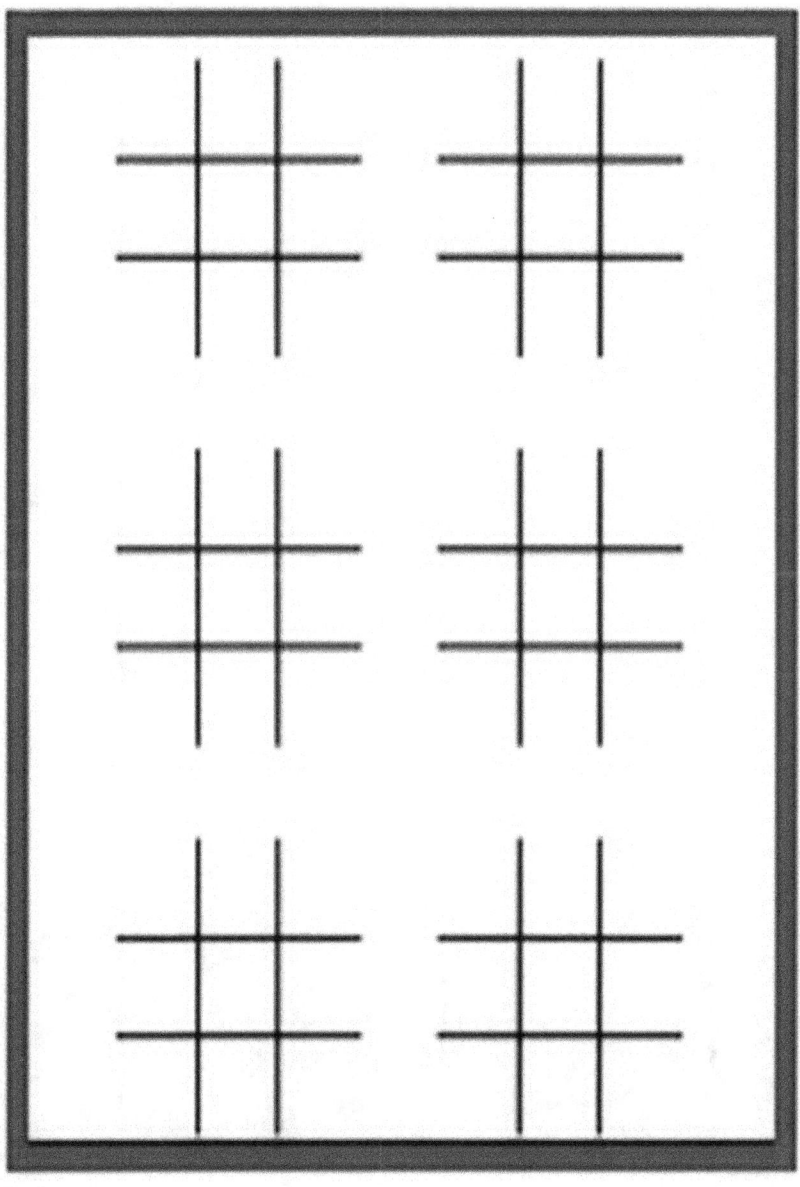

22. Tick Tack Toe Game

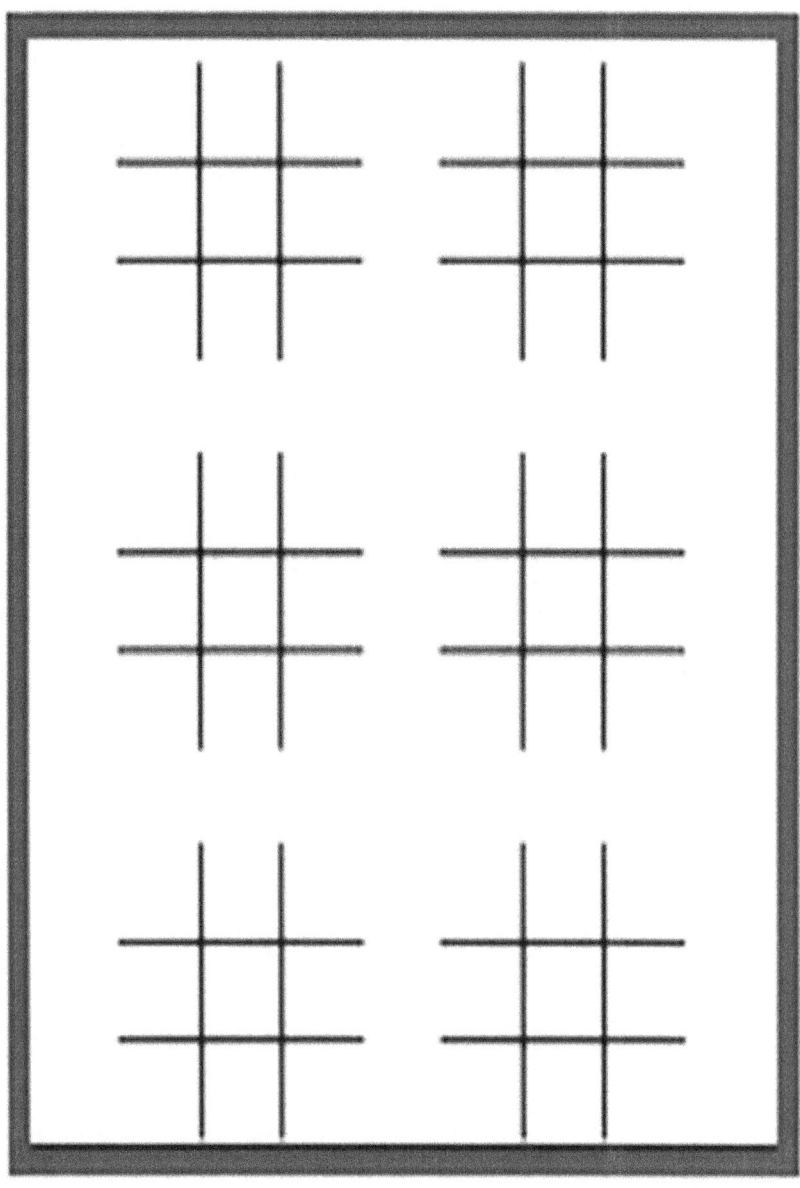

23. Tick Tack Toe Game

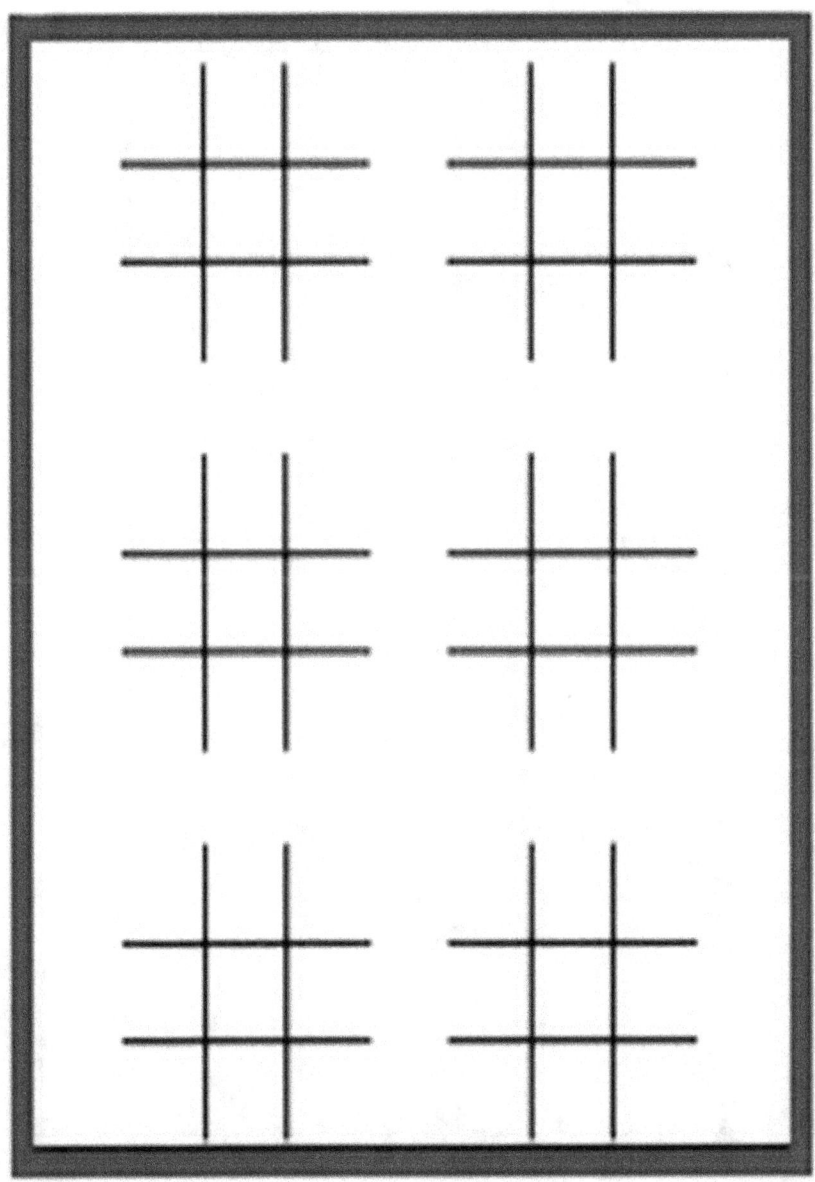

24. Tick Tack Toe Game

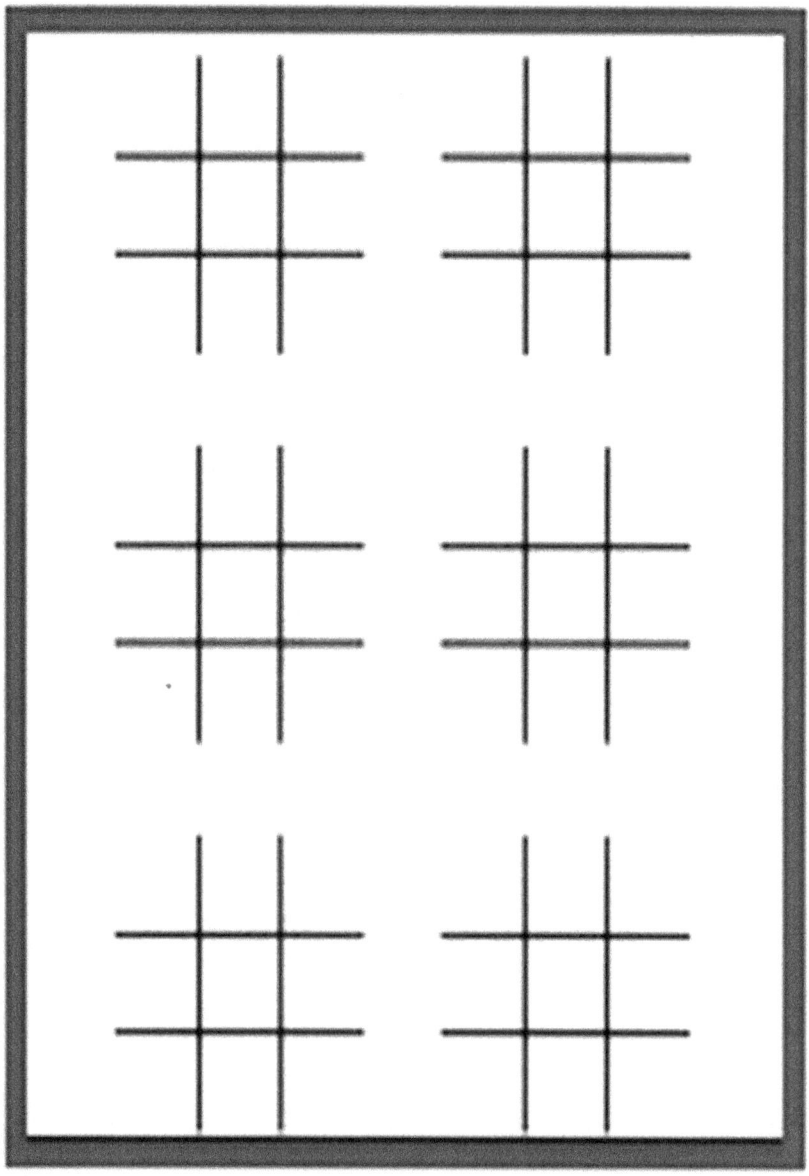

25. Tick Tack Toe Game

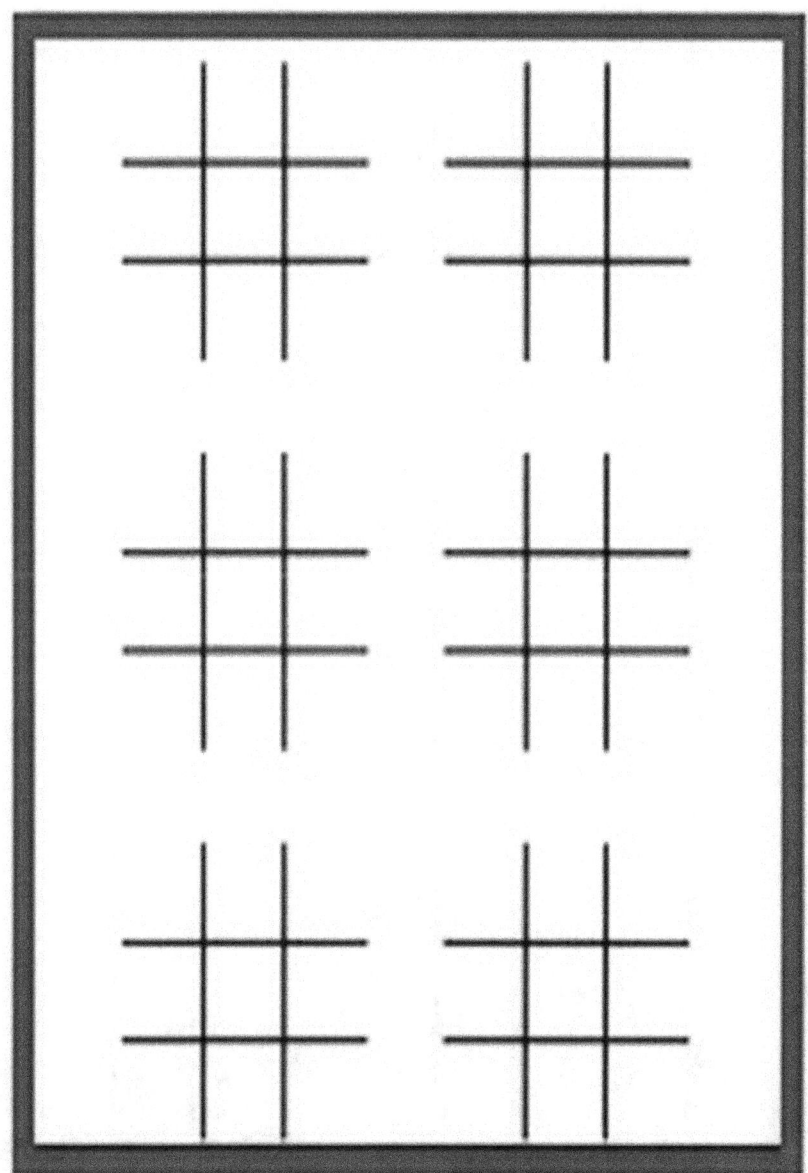

26. Tick Tack Toe Game

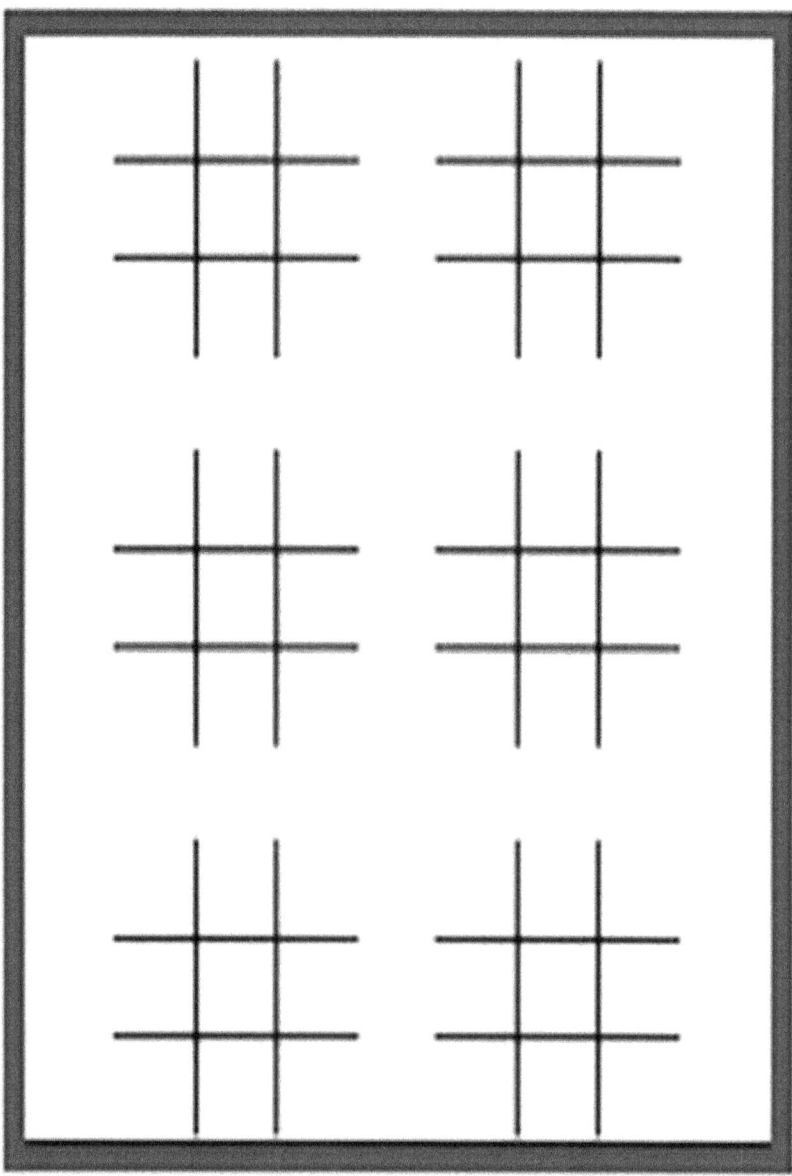

27. Tick Tack Toe Game

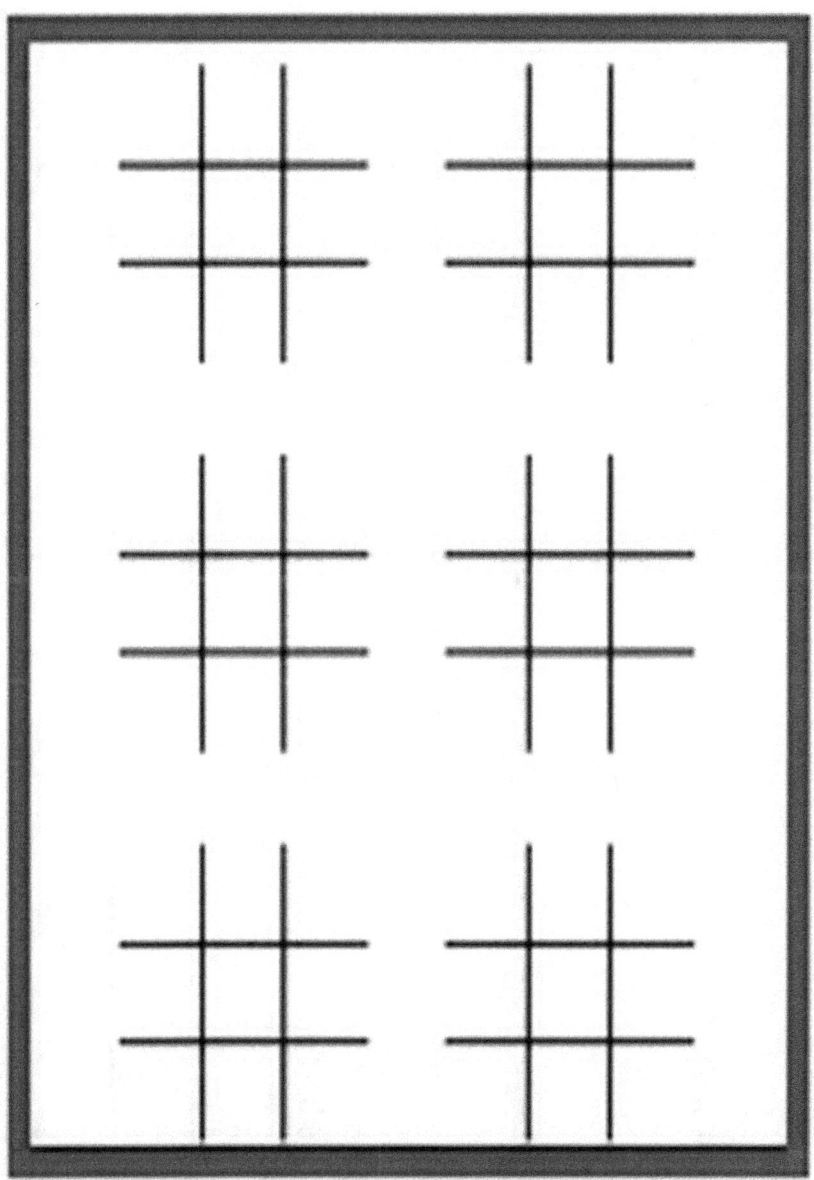

28. Tick Tack Toe Game

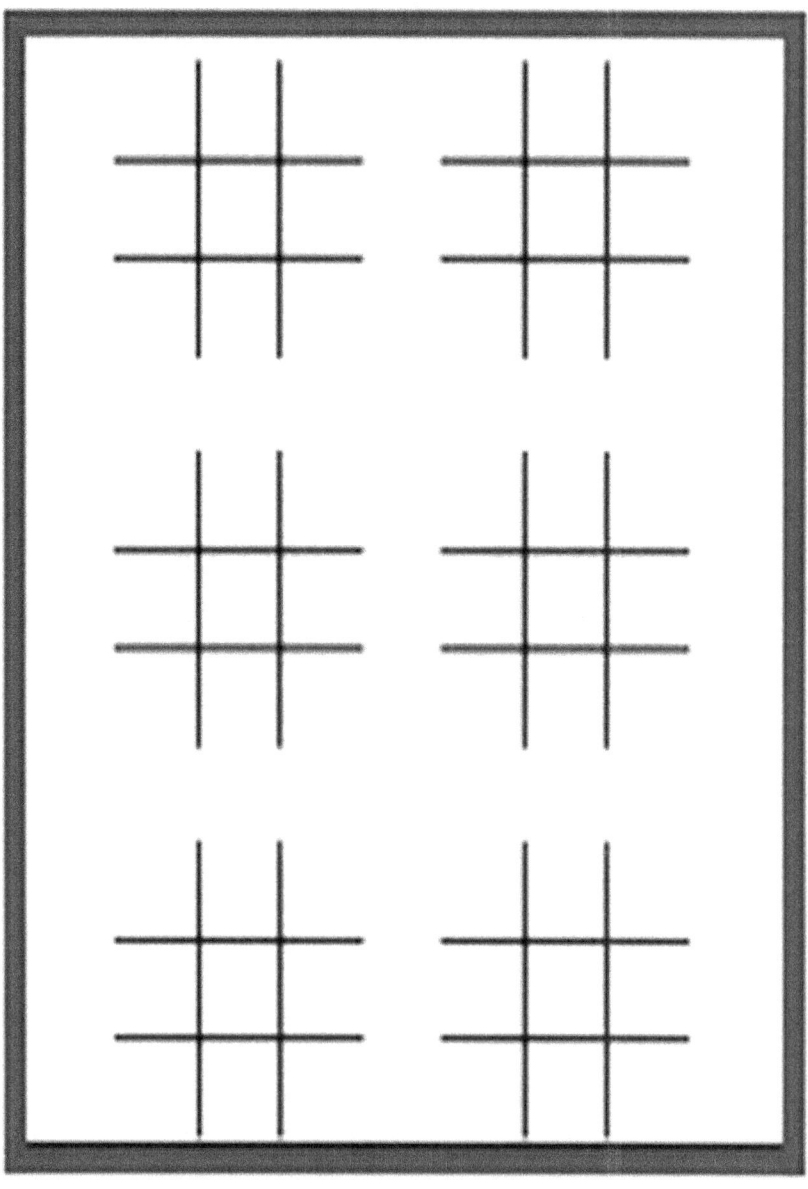

29. Tick Tack Toe Game

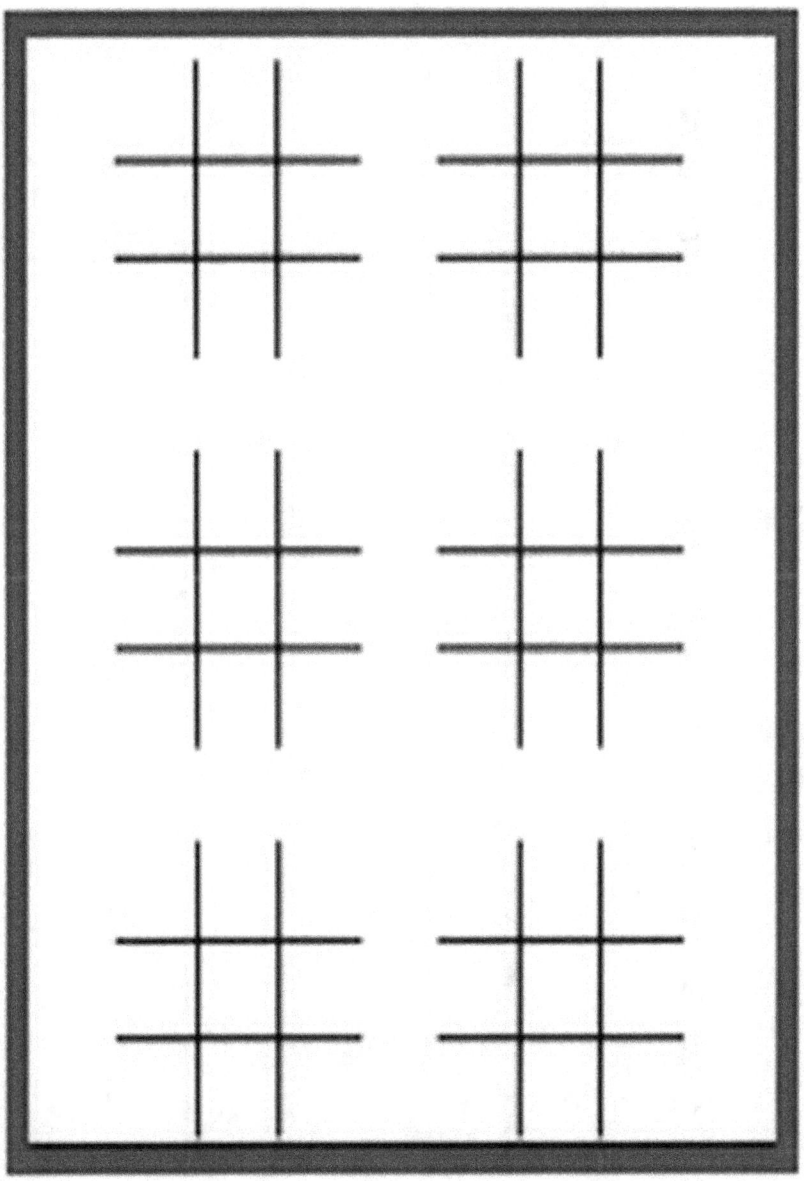

30. Tick Tack Toe Game

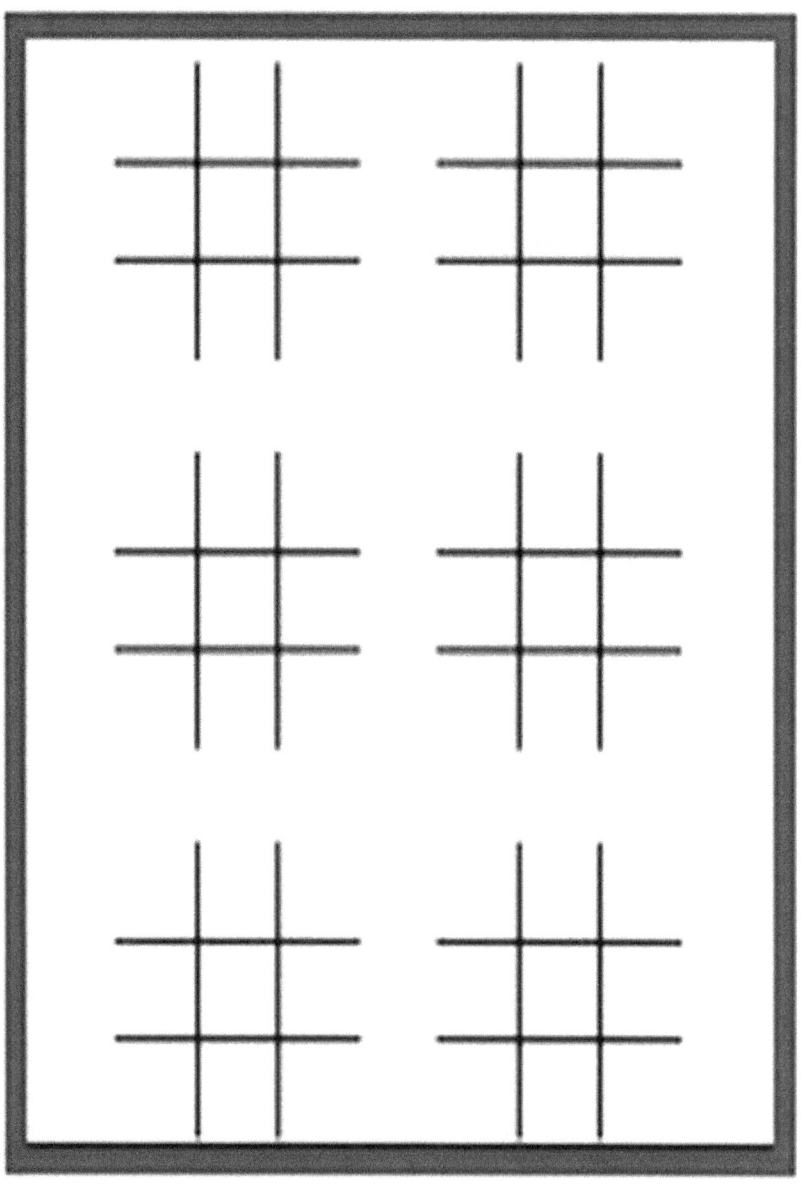

31. Tick Tack Toe Game

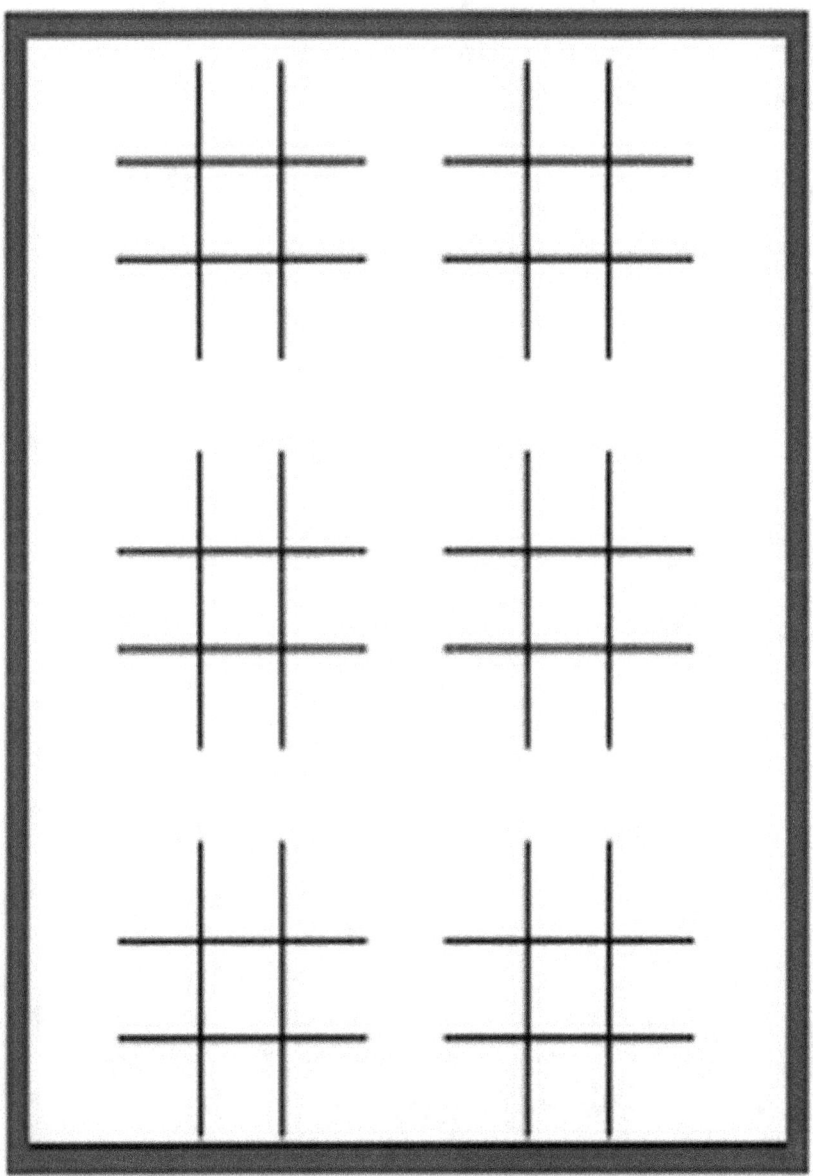

32. In Closing

I want to personally thank everyone for purchasing my Tick Tack Toe Game book and hope you and your family will enjoy.

Art

www.ingramcontent.com/pod-product-compliance
Lightning Source LLC
Chambersburg PA
CBHW072029190526
45166CB00015B/1668